THE PREGNANCY GUIDE FOR MEN

2 Books in 1

Become the Perfect Partner with the Complete Handbook to Navigating Pregnancy and Fatherhood for first-Time Dads

By Samson Warner

Copyright

CONTENTS

Book 1: Preparing for the Arrival   5

Introduction   7

Chapter 1: You're Going to be a Dad   11

    Celebrate the News   11

    Get Sentimental   12

    Decide Who and When You're Going to Tell   12

    Double Check Your Benefits   13

    The Next Nine Months   13

Chapter 2: Pregnancy and Mood Swings   17

    Horrible Hormones   17

    How To Deal with Pregnancy Mood Swings   19

Chapter 3: Be Her Hero   23

    The First Trimester   23

    The Second Trimester   27

    The Third Trimester   30

Chapter 4: You Matter Too   37

    Stick to a Routine   37

    Manage Your Responsibilities   38

    Stand Up for Yourself   38

    Blow Off Some Steam   38

Conclusion   41

References   42

Book 2: Navigating the Newborn Phase   43

Introduction   45

Chapter 1: The First Few Weeks   47

    Day 1   50

    Day 2   51

    Day 3   51

Day 4   52

Day 5   53

Dealing with Emotions   53

Chapter 2: Balancing Life and Fatherhood   59

Take Some Time Off   59

Work-Life Balance   60

Re-Classify Your Relationship   60

Take Care of Your Emotional Health   61

The Nitty Gritty   63

Extra Tips for Hands-On Dads   65

Chapter 3: Bond with Your Baby   67

Tips for Creating Secure Attachment   69

Challenges to Bonding with Your Baby   74

Conclusion   77

References   79

Book 1
Preparing for the Arrival

A Comprehensive and Practice Guide
for Expectant Fathers

INTRODUCTION

You recently found out your partner is expecting, what now? If you're anything like me, the moment after your wife or significant other told you the news, you were hit by random emotions all at once. Joy, happiness, excitement, pride, but also concern, self-doubt, and apprehension. What a confusing time.

Many doubts are running through your head. "Will I be a good dad?" "Are we financially prepared to give our little one all they may need?" Saying you're having sleepless nights is an understatement; your whole day is consumed with worry. There's one question that I know is popping up regularly and that is, "What can I do to support my partner as she grows our baby inside her?"

It's no secret that the next nine months are going to be a rollercoaster. Not only will your partner go through changes that will affect her physically and mentally, but you're both going to prepare to welcome a new life into your home. If not approached correctly, this process will put strain on your marriage.

Soon-to-be dads and moms often announce, *"We're* pregnant," and that is how you should deal with what lies ahead. You have a role to play in your wife's pregnancy and it is one of support and encouragement. Don't get me wrong, you're going to have your down days as well, but now is the time to man up and be strong for your wife. You may be struggling with a mix of emotions, but your partner has that to deal with and then some; morning sickness, back ache, sore and swollen feet, are no joke.

As a father, I can tell you that it is more fun to share the load instead of watching from the side-lines. You may not be giving birth, but you have a part to play in the adventure ahead just as you played a part in making this miracle happen.

I'm writing this book to help you avoid making the mistakes I did when my wife was expecting our first child. I'm not going to lie, our first pregnancy experience wasn't the best, as I wasn't actively involved—I didn't know what to do. We ended up fighting more than usual and grew apart in those nine months. It took a lot of work to get back to where we were before we got pregnant. With our second child, I knew I had to change my approach. I had a sit down with my wife and asked her what I did wrong the last time, and how she'd like me to support her now. She reminded me of two very important things, and if you keep this in mind, you will automatically be a more compassionate partner.

First, pregnancy is really hard. It's exhausting and at times, even painful. The nausea, constant headaches, increased hormones mean your wife isn't always going to experience the pregnancy glow people so often talk about. There will be days when she's going to look and feel horrible. On those days, you have to be extra gentle with her. I know you may get annoyed with her complaining about the same things over and over again, but she has a right to—she's pregnant for nine months.

Secondly, your partner is scared. This is especially true if they're a first-time mom. They're venturing into unknown territory, and just like you have your worries, they have theirs. The good thing is that often, your and her fears are the same, which creates a space for you two to connect and support each other.

If your wife has been pregnant before, this doesn't necessarily mean that she'll worry less. She may have a better idea of what pregnancy is like and how life will be after giving birth, but she's still terrified of all the things that could go wrong with the growing baby in her belly.

I was surprised when my wife told me that one of her main worries was that I would grow to hate her and our relationship would fail; of course, my detached attitude didn't help to allay her fears. You may not think so at the time, but your wife doesn't want to be moody, reactive, overly criticizing, and nit-picky. My wife explained that she would often feel like she was going crazy after her emotional outbursts, followed by a large amount of guilt for treating me poorly. Knowing this, instead of reacting negatively towards her, I saw the situation for what it was and reacted with compassion, instead of getting defensive.

It's safe to say that our second pregnancy was one filled with encouragement, togetherness, and growth because we took the time to sit down and talk about our needs. I'm not sure how things would've turned out if I did not put in the effort to be a more supportive partner during my wife's second pregnancy. I don't want you or your partner to go through the same turbulent time, so I decided to write this guide so your love and relationship can grow deeper and you can be a strong unit when your baby arrives. Believe me, it doesn't get any easier after birth, the challenges you face are just different.

In *Pregnancy Guide for Men: Preparing for Fatherhood Before Birth*, you're going to learn what to do when you find out your wife is expecting, what to expect during the pregnancy and how you can support her, but also how you can take care of yourself. You have to find a balance between looking after her and being kind with yourself. As they say, "You can't pour out of an empty cup."

I think it is time we get started, so you can be the man your partner needs during this life-changing experience.

CHAPTER 1: YOU'RE GOING TO BE A DAD

Congratulations! You're soon going to experience the joys of being a father. However, you have an equally important job to do for the next nine months and that is taking care of your wife.

If you just found out you're going to be a parent, there are a few things you need to start doing right away to set the tone for the whole pregnancy. That being said, if you're holding this book because things have gone a little sideways already, don't worry, you can rectify matters and enjoy a more peaceful and joyous pregnancy with your partner.

The first steps to being a supportive parent are:

Celebrate the News

Whether she surprises you with the news or you're with her when those two lines appear, you won't truly know how you're going to react until it happens. Don't be too hard on yourself if you have nothing much to say or no emotion to show. Shock can do that to you. However, once the reality settles in and you've had time to process, show her that you're excited. The hormones surging through your wife's body may already be causing her to overthink, so she may be questioning if you really want a baby after seeing your initial reaction. You have to show her that you're happy about the news sooner rather than later.

When you do think of ways to celebrate, it's best to include your wife when you're making plans. She may not look pregnant yet, but that doesn't mean she's not feeling pregnant. By the time pregnancy is detectable by an at-home pregnancy test, the hormones are strong enough to make her experience early pregnancy symptoms such as extreme tiredness and nausea. She may not be up for going out.

You also have some other things to consider when you're booking a table at a restaurant. Where she once may have loved going to a specific place, she may now have some food aversions that turned a once solid favorite into a nausea-inducing plate of no-no. Of course, neither of you may know this until the waiter brings your order and your wife rushes to the bathroom! You can expect many such revelations in the coming months.

Get Sentimental

I mentioned that she may not feel too secure in herself and your relationship. You can thank the fluctuating hormones for that—you'll soon discover that hormones are the biggest culprit behind many of the hardships that come with being pregnant. So, since she's doubting everything, you need to reassure her that you still love her and will be there for her no matter what. Tell your wife why you fell in love with her. Remind her of some of your favorite things you've done together. Ask her if she remembers your first kiss. It's okay if you get a little sappy and nostalgic to remind her that your love is strong.

The coming months are going to be hard, and it is good to face these unique challenges with a solid foundation. Start reinforcing the base of your relationship now so that you can weather the storms together.

Decide Who and When You're Going to Tell

You may be eager to let the world know that you're going to be a father, but it's not something you can decide to do on your own. I know you have some happy news to share, but your wife may want to wait until after the first trimester. Often, women decide to keep their pregnancy quiet until then in case they have a miscarriage. No one wants to get everyone excited only to later have to share with them such heart-breaking news. That being said, she may be okay with telling a few key people who you both think deserve to know immediately and you know you can trust.

This is something you have to discuss with your partner. It is a very personal decision, so don't go announcing it to the world just yet.

Double Check Your Benefits

What are your company's policies or parental leave? You need to find out if you will still get paid if you take off for your child's birth. By law, you are entitled to 12 week's unpaid paternity leave if you live in the U.S—some companies, however, are nice enough to still pay you a percentage of your salary during this time.

You should also remind your partner to check how her maternity leave works. This will give both of you peace of mind as you'll know what to expect and can plan your finances accordingly.

That covers the immediate steps after finding out you're going to be a father, but before we walk through what lies ahead in detail, there are some general things you should do to take care of your wife during pregnancy.

The Next Nine Months

It's hard to imagine what's lying ahead, but there's one thing you can bank on that is that your life is going to be full of surprises starting now. You'll wake up not knowing if your wife is going to have a good day, or if she's going to struggle with pregnancy brain fog, be overly emotional, have a back more sore than usual, etc.

As they say, "A best defense is a good offense," and if you apply this adage to the next nine months, you and your wife are going to have a significantly better time. In other words, before figuring out how you can be there for your partner depending on how they feel on any particular day, just be there for them. Period.

Below are some of the things I did daily or whenever the need arose, and I kid you not, it fixed most of the issues we had during her first pregnancy. She noticed my effort and felt less alone. If I were you, I'd keep these tips open in your mind—like tabs in an internet browser—and whenever you find yourself at a loss of what to do, quickly scan for an appropriate response.

Lend an Ear

Sometimes, all your partner needs is to vent her worries and frustrations to feel better. Make sure your wife knows that she can talk to you about anything—big or small. Don't just listen when she wants to talk about major things like her fear of being a bad mom; lend an ear when she's irritated with her puffy feet or annoyed because she has a bad craving for pickles dipped in peanut butter, but the shops are closed.

It doesn't matter if you think she's overreacting or being illogical, just listen. She doesn't need you to tell her to "calm down" or "stop worrying." Keep your thoughts to yourself unless you can relate to what she's talking about and feel the need to share. You're a team and you're both experiencing similar fears. Don't hold back on sharing what is going on in your head. She may feel less alone knowing you're struggling too.

Do More Than the Usual

Creating another life will sap the energy out of anyone. Extreme exhaustion is one of the most common pregnancy symptoms. To help lessen the load and give your partner time to rest, pitch in a little more. Help her with household chores and take care of the meal planning and prepping. Do anything that will give her time to put her feet up or take a nap.

As the pregnancy progresses, her baby bump is going to be in the way of most things, sweeping the floor and making the bed is not only going to make her tired but cause a great deal of frustration. So, ask her what chores she's really struggling to do, and take them off of her to-do list entirely until she's given birth and ready to do them again.

Do keep in mind that your partner may want to still do some things for herself. If that's the case, then don't get pushy—help where you can and where she wants and needs you to, but don't try to smother her self-sufficiency.

Get Educated

You may know the basics of pregnancy but now is the time to get even better informed. Reading this book is a great first step to get educated about what is happening to your wife's body as your baby grows. Your partner will appreciate the effort you put into learning all you can about what she's going through. I can't tell you how my wife's face brightened up when I announced our baby was the size of a grapefruit at the moment. Also, the more you know, the less anxious you'll be.

A big part of getting educated is going with your partner to her doctor visits. If you can't make all her prenatal visits, try to accompany her to the milestone appointments where you'll hear your baby's heartbeat for the first time, determine sex, and for important screening tests.

Enrolling for childbirth classes is another great idea to learn a little more about pregnancy and childbirth.

Help Her Stay Healthy

What your wife eats impacts your baby and how she feels while pregnant—a diet filled with junk food is not good for her or the little one. Taking any food aversions into consideration, help your partner eat healthily by serving her wholesome food and snacks. Cravings aside, your wife needs to be conscious of what she's putting into her body to ensure the baby gets all the nutrients and minerals they need to grow.

I also suggest you read up on foods your partner needs to avoid while pregnant. Fish is a good example of something she can't eat due to the high mercury content.

You may also need to help her stay active, which is going to be difficult considering that she's going to feel worn out most of the time. To motivate her, be her workout buddy. Go for walks with her daily or do some light yoga in the garden in the evenings. Find something safe she enjoys and do it with her to encourage her. This time together will also deepen your bond, so it's win-win all around.

Use Your Hands

Once these nine months are over, you'll give a qualified masseuse a run for their money if you give your wife massages as regularly as you should! Her feet are going to kill her, especially the bigger her belly gets. A daily foot rub will make a big difference in bringing down the swelling and making them feel better. But it's not only her feet you should be taking care of; your wife's back and shoulders will benefit from a massage too. It's not necessarily about rubbing out knots but about comforting her with your touch. Of course, back massages can quickly turn steamy if the mood strikes, so you may want to explore some new sex positions she'll be comfortable in.

When it comes to sex, men are often concerned that they'll hurt the baby. You have nothing to worry about. Your little one is safely tucked away in the uterus, and they'll have no idea what is going on. The only person you have to worry about is your wife, so make sure that she feels comfortable throughout.

Don't Take Things Too Seriously

This is not the time to lose your sense of humor or take things too seriously. You will have to learn how to deal with getting sudden and strange food requests just as you sit down to watch your favorite TV show after a day filled with chores. You'll have to be okay with stopping for a pee break for the umpteenth time when you're driving long distance. There are many things that are going to annoy you and if you don't practice compassion, you may lash out at your partner and she doesn't deserve that. Instead, look for the humor in each situation. Who knows, all these odd pregnancy adventures may turn into funny stories you can tell your child.

CHAPTER 2: PREGNANCY AND MOOD SWINGS

Let's establish one thing: At the end of this pregnancy, you're going to hate hormones.

Your wife is going to have major fluctuations in her mood all thanks to the hormones surging through her body. In fact, at times, it may feel to you as if she is a walking mood swing. You may feel like everything you do annoys her, and you know what? It probably does. Not a thing you do is right and there's nothing you can do about it. Your only recourse is to say, "Yes dear," and be there for her.

Horrible Hormones

Before we look at other ways you can deal with your wife's instability—and I mean that in the kindest way possible—let's name the hormones responsible for all the chaos.

Culprit #1: Human Chorionic Gonadotropin (HCG)

If you've ever wondered how an at-home-pregnancy test works, this hormone is responsible for that second line showing up. Some would argue that HCG is the most important hormone during pregnancy as it tells the body to create a safe space for the baby to grow. Your partner will also stop producing eggs each month thanks to the surge of this hormone. During the early stage of pregnancy, HCG will double every second day until it peaks at 60-90 days.

Culprit #2: Estrogen and Progesterone

Of all the hormones running through your wife's body, you can thank these two for making her and your life unbearable the next coming months. These hormones are responsible for all the unwanted pregnancy symptoms that expecting mothers have to endure.

Tiredness: Progesterone has the same effect as sleeping tablets. The problem is that your wife can't decide to just take it before getting some sleep; she will experience it throughout the day.

Breast sensitivity: The first semester is the worst when it comes to breast sensitivity because estrogen and progesterone levels are especially high during this time.

Hip pain: Progesterone softens cartilage to prepare the pubic bone for giving birth. This leads to sore hips, which makes moving around pretty uncomfortable.

Bloating: This is one of the most common pregnancy symptoms. Progesterone has a muscle relaxing effect, which causes swelling as the bowel muscles are too relaxed to keep the gas from pushing outward.

Reflux and heartburn: I mentioned that progesterone relaxes muscles. Unfortunately, it's not able to target muscles, which means all her smooth muscles can be affected. This means that even her esophageal sphincter may have too much slack, increasing acid reflux and heartburn. Also, as your baby's living quarters get too large later in pregnancy, it may press against her stomach, pushing up acid, which will make an already uncomfortable situation worse.

One good thing about these hormones is that they may trigger what is known as "nesting" at some stage, where your wife won't be able to stop herself from cleaning—everything! During this time, you may get a reprieve from doing all the housework. But beware; she may have the need to throw away some of your stuff she thinks are cluttering up the place!

When the levels of hormones drop after your baby is born, you're going to have to be even stronger than you were the past nine months. The slump in hormones along with the stress and fatigue of giving birth, your wife may reach a new level of moodiness. She may develop postnatal depression, which we'll look at a little later in this chapter. Whether she's just extra moody or has baby blues, with a bit of understanding and patience, she'll be back to her pre-pregnancy self in no time.

Culprit #3: Relaxin

Relaxin does exactly what its name implies: relaxes. Much like progesterone, this hormone helps loosen ligaments in the pelvic region to prepare for birth. Although a relaxed pelvic bone will make it easier for a baby to pass through, it causes pain in the hips while moving around with an extra large belly.

Culprit #4: Oxytocin

This is known as the love hormone. Affection triggers this hormone in men and women, but when pregnant, it signals a female's body to go into labor. When a doctor wants to induce labor, they usually inject a synthetic form of oxytocin called Pitocin. This hormone, however, doesn't only get produced at the end of pregnancy, but in tiny amounts throughout to help stretch the cervix and prepare the breasts to produce milk.

Culprit #5: Prolactin

Although oxytocin also prompts milk production, prolactin is the main hormone responsible for repairing beast tissue for lactation. Prolactin is 10 to 20 times higher during pregnancy than other times, and at such a high amount, it has a tranquilizing effect, which contributes to your pregnant partner's fatigue.

How To Deal with Pregnancy Mood Swings

You now know more about the hormones at play in your wife's body, but that's not the type of knowledge that's going to help you deal with the related moodiness. To survive this emotional roller-coaster ride you're on with your partner, you will have to learn how to deal with her moods in an effective way. Here's how:

Tolerance is Key

This is probably the most important tip I can give you. Be patient. You are going to get irritated and frustrated, but you have to do whatever you can to manage your emotions. Keep reminding yourself that her bad mood won't last forever and that you just need to stand strong until her mood lifts. If you don't teach yourself to be tolerant, your days will be filled with screaming battles.

Forget Any Logic

The words "rational" and "pregnancy" don't always go together. When your partner is at her moodiest, logic and rationalism go out the window. Although you may want to correct her, just let it go. Now is not the time for being right; it's about being flexible in how you handle matters for your wife's sake.

Don't Respond in Anger

Crying, yelling, or getting irritated for no apparent reason at all has a tendency to happen throughout pregnancy. It's during these times that you have to remind yourself that this is the hormones talking and not your wife. If you approach it this way, it will be easier for you to respond with love and not in anger.

Make Her Feel Special

A growing belly and puffy and swollen feet don't really encourage feeling sexy. She won't be able to fit into that little black dress she knows you like so much, and that is going to contribute to her feeling unattractive and fat. To make her feel better, let her know you still find her beautiful and you'll love her no matter how her body changes during and after pregnancy.

Plan a Date Night

Spending quality time together will be a welcome distraction from the worries and challenges you two are experiencing. Make plans to go out and enjoy yourselves. You can visit some of your favorite places—if she can still stomach the food—or you can go for a picnic, a movie, or spoil her for a couple's spa day.

Remember, It's Not About You

You're standing there getting yelled at and you have no idea why. Worse yet, the reasons she's giving for her discontent are minor, non-issues, which doesn't warrant such an intense outburst. It's easy to start to believe that you're doing something wrong if you're constantly told that you are. Again, remind yourself that it's not her, it is the hormones talking, and you shouldn't take it personally.

Mood swings can wreak havoc on relationships, and if you take all the negative things she's saying to heart, it is going to lead to unhappiness on your part. This can quickly spiral and before you know it, your relationship is on shaky grounds.

I know this chapter may have been a bit of a wake-up call to many of you. It can be jarring to read that your wife is going to transform into someone you don't know or necessarily like. The most important thing I want you to take from what you've read so far is that your wife cannot control her hormones, but you can control the way you respond to what they make her do.

In the next chapter, we're going to take your wife's pregnancy and break it down week by week. This way you'll know exactly what to expect, and you can prepare accordingly.

CHAPTER 3: BE HER HERO

I t's time to familiarize you with what is waiting for you, your partner, and your growing bundle of joy. I made sure to throw in some interesting facts you can share with your wife throughout the process, so that she can see you're eager to learn about what is going on in her belly.

So, let's get you educated (and excited)!

The First Trimester

I'm going to have to confuse you for a minute—believe me, it took me much longer to wrap my head around what I'm going to tell you.

Your wife's pregnancy includes two weeks when she's not actually pregnant. Weeks one and two are when she's meant to ovulate; in other words, release the egg that your sperm should fertilize to create a baby. During ovulation, the egg breaks free from the ovary and finds its way down the fallopian tube and into her uterus. Along the way, it needs to collide with a sperm for a baby to happen.

If you're trying to conceive, these two weeks are go-time! You need to have sex regularly to increase the chances of becoming pregnant. You wife most probably already know about tracking her cycle and using ovulation tests to pin-point when exactly her egg will be released. If not, do some research with her to find out what you both can do to get pregnant naturally.

Now that you understand why we're only starting at the three-week mark with discovering what is going on with your partner and baby, it is time to marvel at how great your wife's body is at creating a new human.

Week 3

Baby on board! One of your little swimmers was successful and fertilized your wife's egg. What once was a single cell is now swiftly separating into a tiny ball of cells that will in nine months greet you and the world.

Your wife won't have any pregnancy symptoms yet, so she won't know what is happening inside her. For those of you who are actively trying to fall pregnant, the two weeks between ovulation and your wife's next menstrual cycle is going to feel like a month. Instead of wondering if she's pregnant or not, and constantly thinking about what may be going on in her tummy, take your mind off of things. Let nature do what nature does best, while you go on with your lives.

Week 4

Around now, your wife may be considering taking a pregnancy test if this is a planned pregnancy. It's a bit too soon and the chance of getting a false negative is higher at this time. To prepare for a possible positive result, why not get rid of unhealthy habits? I quit smoking because I was afraid the second-hand smoke would harm mommy and baby, and my wife ditched overly-processed foods (for the most part) and focused on eating a wholesome diet. After the pregnancy, we both were in better physical shape, which was a blessing—running after a tiny tot who is exploring their world is extremely tiring.

For those of you who aren't actively working toward having a baby, you may be none the wiser about being pregnant, but that is going to change soon…

Week 5

Your wife may be showing some early pregnancy symptoms like achy breasts and extreme tiredness. There's one problem: Premenstrual stress (PMS) has the same symptoms, so she may be writing it off as her period approaching. The only way to know if she's pregnant is to take a pregnancy test. Luckily, HCG is starting to climb and will be detectable on at-home-pregnancy tests from now on. If you get a positive result, congratulations! Your baby is as tiny as an orange seed right about now.

One of the first chores you'll have to take over from now on is cleaning out the litter box if you have a cat. Your wife and baby are at risk of toxoplasmosis, a disease that's spread through parasites in cat poop. Although rare, it's better to be safe than sorry.

Week 6

Morning sickness usually starts right about now, but as you'll soon find out, calling it "morning sickness" is deceptive. Nausea can hit at any time of the day; in fact, many pregnant women feel queasy the entire day!

When your wife's stomach is empty, her nausea may feel even worse. This is where you come in; make sure she eats regularly. If she finds it difficult to eat full meals, cheese and crackers will do, as long as she gets something into her tummy to feel better. Smoothies are a great option for those days when she feels extra woozy and can't get herself to eat anything solid.

Week 7

Another interesting pregnancy symptom is poking out its nose this week, and that is an increased sense of smell. Your cologne, a scent say may have loved before falling pregnant, may send her running to the bathroom. Your wife is a bloodhound at this point, so don't question her when she says there's a dead mouse under the couch; it's there, believe me!

Week 8

Food aversions are really kicking in right about now. It's up to you to find healthy foods to replace the ones she can't stomach any longer. It's going to be hit or miss, but don't give up. As long as you're switching them out for foods high in baby-building goodness, then you're on the right track. Even if she eats it today but hates it the next, she'll still be getting in all the nutrients she needs if her food choices are healthy.

Week 9

Your wife's breasts may start to get tender around about now, and her nipples are growing larger. It may be so sore that even material rubbing against her breasts will cause major discomfort. Now is not the time to get kinky in the bedroom and bring out the nipple clamps. Even the slightest touch may be too much for her, so be gentle.

Week 10

It's time for the first of many prenatal check-ups. Clear your schedule and go with her. There's nothing that brings two people together as seeing (and hearing) what they've created together. Accompanying her to the doctor's visits will also give you insight into what is going on in her body.

Attending these check-ups isn't just good for your wife. You'll look back at experiencing milestones such as hearing your baby's heartbeat or discovering their gender, and it will bring a smile to your face. Being a present dad doesn't start after your child is born; it beings while your little one is still developing.

If you can't make the appointment, try to video call so that you're still a part of it even though you're not there in flesh and bone.

Week 11

You'll be just out the door and you'll have to open up for your wife to go to the toilet, even though she just went. Not only are her kidneys more efficient at their job, but the hormones are causing an almost constant flow of urine. Don't be surprised when you find her getting up to go to the bathroom at least two to three times a night.

To keep her safe and avoid any dangerous falls, DIY some solutions to light up her path to the toilet. Also make sure that there's no furniture or clutter in her way.

Week 12

You may start to notice that your wife isn't in the mood to have sex very often any more. Don't take it personally. She's tired, nauseous, and bloated, and making love is the last thing on her mind. Luckily, there's more than one way to be intimate. Grab some snacks and cuddle up in bed to watch a movie, or hold hands as you go for a stroll in the park.

There are women who won't be able to have enough sex while pregnant. They're insatiable. If your wife falls in this category, enjoy it while it lasts because it is extremely difficult to get time to make love after the baby is born.

Week 13

You made it a third of the way! Your wife is in the last week of her first trimester and there's only six months left to go. Your baby has also come a long way; they're the size of a lemon now.

You may notice that your wife is discussing her pregnancy with her girlfriend or family members more than with you. There's a good explanation for that: She doesn't want to bore you. She's been talking about the pregnancy nonstop, and she's afraid you'll lose interest. It's up to you to reassure you that you're with her every step of the way and even if she tells you the same thing over and over, you still want to hear it.

The Second Trimester

I have some good news, your life with a hormonally-driven pregnant woman is going to get significantly easier from now on as many of the pregnancy symptoms start to ease up somewhat. Your wife's energy is starting to return, she won't have to pee so often, and her breasts aren't as sensitive as they were during the first trimester. My wife especially enjoyed this part of pregnancy as you could start to see her baby bump. I remember she was so excited when she could see she was pregnant and not just bloated.

Let's look at what else is in store for you in the next 14 weeks.

Week 14

Your partner has been complaining of pregnancy symptoms for a long time, so don't be surprised if you start to experience them yourself! Sympathetic pregnancy (also known as couvade syndrome) does happen, and you may find yourself getting green at the gills when you smell scrambled eggs, or find yourself craving a double-thick chocolate milkshake at 2 am (Syndrome, n.d.).

Your wife may be starting to have sharp pains in her abdomen, which can be quite alarming! This is just another pregnancy symptom called round ligament pain and is caused by ligaments stretching as her uterus grows (Healthline, 2016). She'll feel it most when she suddenly gets up or changes positions too quickly. Coughing and sneezing can also cause these pregnancy growing pains.

To help her, place a pillow under her feet to help relieve the strain on her ligaments caused by a heavier uterus.

Week 15

Now may be the time to brainstorm some baby names. Get a pen and paper, grab your partner by the hand and get cozy on the couch—this may take a while. Taking the initiative to be involved in this important part of having a baby will make your wife's heart melt. You've probably already touched on the subject, but narrowing things down or even deciding on a name makes everything more real.

Make your way through the alphabet and write down options you really like. You can even get creative and mix and match your and your wife's names or family names.

Week 16

Your wife may be struggling with the fact that she is gaining weight. Although she's well aware that there's a fantastic reason for her growing tummy, she's going to find it difficult nonetheless and you're going to have to help her embrace her new shape. If planned correctly, taking her shopping may boost her mood if she finds clothes she feels good in. Of course, if you don't think this through and you take her to a place that doesn't sell maternity wear, she may walk out sobbing and that's not the reaction you want.

Also, remind your partner that as long as she's eating nutrient-dense foods and exercising, the weight she's putting on is healthy and nothing to worry or be ashamed about. She should think of every pound extra as an indication of a healthy, growing baby.

Week 17

Pregnancy stuffs up a lot of things and your partner's nose is no exception. This means your wife may turn into the world-champion of snoring overnight. The good news is that it is only temporary. See it this way, it's her time to give you a good dose of your own medicine!

To help quiet things down, you can put a humidifier in the room or buy her some nasal strips to keep the air flowing freely. If that doesn't work, you may want to sleep on the couch a few nights a week to get some shut eye.

To make you both feel better about the snoring situation, I think it's time for another "wow" fact. The swirls, grooves, and lines totally individual to your baby are starting to form on their fingertips and toes anytime from now. Cool, right?

Weeks 18 & 19

Sitting, standing, or lying down, your partner's back is going to hurt no matter what. Her entire center of gravity is shifting due to her uterus growing in size—basically, her tummy is so heavy it is pulling her forward. This puts a lot of strain on her back. Add to that the increase of relaxin—the pregnancy hormone we talked about earlier—and backaches are going to be in the picture for the foreseeable future.

Help your wife out by getting her a footrest so that her feet are always elevated while sitting. A warm bath also works wonders so stock up on bubble bath and make sure you have a nice and hot bath ready for her in the evening. As an extra treat, pour her a glass of non-alcoholic bubbly and place some healthy snacks in reach and you'll be her hero for sure.

Weeks 20 & 21

It's time for your baby's anatomy scan, and if you're lucky, you'll be able to see whether it's a boy or a girl. This is one doctor's appointment you don't want to miss. It is an important exam, which will give your doctor a clear idea of how everything is going and growing.

Talking about growing, your baby is going to leave their mark anytime from now—in the form of stretch marks, and your partner is not going to be too happy about it. Surprise her with tissue oil or a lotion rich in vitamin E to help combat pregnancy scars.

Weeks 22 & 23

Your partner's tummy isn't the only thing growing at the 22-23-week mark. If you've been giving her foot rubs as diligently as you should, you may have noticed that her feet feel larger. You're not wrong, a pregnant woman's feet can actually go up a shoe size during pregnancy. Great reason to take her shoe shopping. Of course, you may have to remind her that the stilettos will have to wait until later; for now, comfort is key.

Weeks 24 & 25

Your baby's hearing has been developing quite remarkably. In fact, they can hear so well that they'll be able to recognize your and their mom's voice after birth. You can use this as an excuse for some family bonding! Make a playlist for your little one and introduce them to all you and your wife's favorite songs. You may want to avoid singing along if you're more of a shower singer—you don't want to hurt your baby's ears. Choosing the right music now, may turn into tunes you can use to put them asleep later on.

Weeks 26 & 27

The end of the second trimester is in sight, which means the big day is fast approaching. With that realization, comes a lot of questions and concerns. Labor day may be a recurring topic of discussion starting now, so help ease your wife's nerves by reading up about it as much as you can. You may even want to organize a tour of the hospital and delivery room, so that she'll feel more relaxed. Childbirth classes are also a great option.

If you're looking for something goofy to take your wife's mind off of labor, grab a flashlight! Your baby's eyes are beginning to open, but since they don't have a room with a view, you can entertain them for a short while by shining a flashlight at your wife's stomach. Don't go too close or your wife might get a kick in response when things become a little too bright.

The Third Trimester

You may not think your wife's tummy can grow any larger, but believe me, it is going to get a lot bigger in the third trimester. Your baby is going to go from two and a half pounds and 16 inches long, to between six and nine pounds and 19 to 22 inches. Their living space is getting smaller and smaller and that causes a lot of issues for mommy—getting your vital organs kicked every so often isn't very pleasant.

Thankfully, you're in the homestretch now and before you know it, you'll be holding your angel in your arms. Until then, don't plan any trips; you want to be close to the hospital of choice when the big day comes. Air travel is also off limits from 36 weeks, so a staycation is your best option.

Here's what you have to look forward to for the remainder of the pregnancy.

Weeks 28 & 29

Only two more months to go! As you can imagine, it's getting pretty cramped in there, so your wife will have to start doing kick counts. From the 28-week mark, you need to remind your partner to monitor your baby's movements daily to make sure everything is A-okay. All your wife needs to do is to sit or lie down and count all the movements she feels until she gets to 10. If an hour has passed and she doesn't feel 10 flutters or kicks, bring her a light snack and check if baby gets active after the blood sugar spike. If your little one doesn't move at least 10 times in two hours, reach out to your health practitioner. It may be nothing, but it's best to double check just in case.

Weeks 30 & 31

I have bad news. The first trimester pregnancy symptoms you were so happy to see go, are on their way back. Your wife's need to pee constantly, sore breasts, fatigue, and heartburn will pay her a visit for a second time and stay for the remainder of her pregnancy. A lot is going on in her body to prepare for delivery, as well as feeding your little one afterward, so expect some discomfort.

One thing that won't be uncomfortable is having sex, and I hope you've been doing it throughout her pregnancy. If you have, your wife may have noticed that your baby quiets down, probably due to the rocking motion, or they become extra active to join the party. Both these reactions are normal, and you shouldn't let it deter you from being intimate.

Weeks 32 to 35

Your little one is getting ready to make their debut. In general, babies weigh around three and a half to four pounds right about now. Your wife may be experiencing strange movements from your baby as their once comfy home starts to feel a little too cramped. They should also be getting into position anytime from now to prepare for their journey through the birth canal, so that may explain the extra squirming.

It's also at this time that the Braxton Hicks contractions will begin, leading to a lot of panic and confusion (Healthline, 2019). Think of these contractions as a practice run for the real thing. They're easy to misjudge for labor contractions, especially for first-time parents. If you're not sure, ask your wife to change position. Braxton Hicks contractions will go away if she gets up to walk after sitting, for example. A warm bath is a good way to take the edge off of these imposter contractions.

Weeks 36 to 39

It's almost time for all systems go! Your baby is doing their bit inside the womb to prepare for their ETA. One of the biggest changes they're going through is preparing their lungs for their first breath, but don't discount all the other small but equally important changes like their brain and nervous system getting ready to deal with the wonderful world that awaits them.

If you haven't packed your wife's hospital bag yet, then don't wait a minute longer. Your baby may decide to be an early bloomer or they may decide to be fashionably late. Whatever the case may be, you need to be prepared.

Your wife may be extra needy at the moment, and so may you. That's okay. Comfort each other. The emotional ups and downs you both are going to experience in the coming days necessitates being there for eachother. Soon, the pregnancy hardships will be a distant memory.

Weeks 40 to 42

Your wife is officially at the end of her pregnancy even though she may not have given birth yet. Your baby is ready to come out and say, "Hi" to mommy and daddy, but maybe your partner's body isn't quite there yet. You may have circled their due date in bright red on the calendar, but that's only an estimate if your partner wants to give birth naturally. So, it's going to be a waiting game.

If your baby is late, you both may start to worry about their health and well-being. You don't have to. Your wife's doctor will keep a close eye on your baby and will run all the necessary tests to make sure they're just biding their time, and nothing is wrong. I do recommend you start to consider the fact that giving birth naturally may not be the best option anymore. At week 42, your bundle of joy is the size of a big, juicy watermelon, so opting for a C-section may be the better choice.

Dos and Don'ts in the Delivery Room

There's not much I can say to prepare you for this day. Your dad friends have probably already told you of their experience in the delivery room and some of their stories may have left your eyes wide and your jaw on the floor.

One thing is certain, you may have planned everything out perfectly, but more times than not, you'll need to rethink and adapt to the circumstances. That being said, it is better to create a birth plan with your wife, so that all decisions made are according to you and the mother of your child's wants and needs.

When your doctor and pregnancy team are aware of what you expect from them, you don't have to worry about advocating for your wife and yourself; you can focus on providing the emotional support your partner needs during labor.

I know you're wondering what "emotional support" entails, so let me help you by laying out some delivery room etiquette.

Talk about what your wife expects from you in the delivery room.
You're going to talk about labor day—a lot! During one of these occasions, remember to ask your wife what she expects of you. Emotions are already running high, so putting your foot in it by supporting her in a way that she finds annoying, is not going to end well. Take the time to find out what she sees as supportive behavior. Ask her if she wants you to rub her back or hold her hand during, or would she prefer it if you don't touch her at all. Of course, all of this may change when the day comes; where she said she doesn't want you to hold her hand, she may suddenly grab yours and cling to it for dear life. Be willing to adapt to her needs.

Don't pull a face.

You're going to see a lot of things in the delivery room. Some of these things you may wish to unsee. I know managing your facial expressions isn't easy, especially when you're overwhelmed and stressed at the moment, but you have to do your best to keep your expression neutral. Your partner is probably going to look at you throughout the process as a way to gauge what is going on "down there." Don't give her reason to worry. Furthermore, you don't want your wife to feel self-conscious, so keep your shock and horror for yourself.

Know what you can handle.

Don't walk into the delivery room thinking your normally-queasy stomach will now all of the sudden be able to handle blood and gore. I know you want to be there for her, but she has enough to worry about. Your fainting is going to distract her from her main goal: giving birth to your baby. Honor your limits. There's nothing wrong standing next to your wife's shoulder instead of taking a front-row seat. You're there; you're participating in the process in a way that is true to you. Now is not the time to be macho and miss out on your baby's birth because you fainted at the sight of blood.

Don't show her how nervous you are.

Stay calm. Do some breathing exercises and think positive and peaceful thoughts. Your energy needs to scream tranquility and composure. I know it's a stressful experience, but your wife needs you to be her rock right now.

Come prepared.

There are some items you just have to have with you while your wife is giving birth. A washcloth is great to wipe away and sweat and cool down her forehead; a hair tie will come in handy to put her hair up and out of her face; chapstick will keep her lips from cracking should she get dehydrated from all the moaning. For you, take a vomit bag and I'm not even kidding. Nevermind the sights and sounds, the stress and excitement alone are enough to trigger you to throw up.

Don't tell her to, "Just breathe."

There's more to it than just breathing. Your partner may be taking too many shallow breaths, too fast, which can lead to her hyperventilating. If you tell her to just breathe at that moment, she'll just continue to do what she's doing or may even do it faster. What you can do instead is to put your hand on their chest, look into their eyes, and demonstrate how to breathe; take deep and slow breaths until she mimics you and her breathing calms down.

Rest.

Giving birth is not a quick one, two, three for most women; it can last anything from a few hours to days. Even though your wife may pass out from exhaustion in between contractions, you may find it more difficult to fall asleep because you're too worried about her or you don't want to miss the big moment. To avoid this, make a plan before she goes into labor about how you're going to manage your sleep. If you're a deep sleeper, consider setting a timer to wake up and check on your wife every hour. If you're still nervous that you may sleep through the birth of your child, relax, the doctor or nurses will wake you when they see it is time.

This is a mammoth chapter, filled with a lot of important information you need to process. However, it's impossible to remember what your wife is going through week by week. I recommend you make this chapter your go-to throughout the pregnancy. On a Sunday, go to the corresponding week/s ahead, and recap what you and she can expect, and what you can do to support her. This is just a small way you can make sure you're there for her in a way that matters.

In the next chapter, we're going to shift focus a little by looking at your needs during this time. The reality is that you can't pour from an empty cup, so it is crucial that you take care of your stress levels and health if you want to be there for her.

It's true that your partner and baby should be the center of your attention, but I want you to put yourself first (occasionally) for your own sanity. That may sound at odds with the whole message of this book so far, but ultimately, looking after yourself plays a big role in being able to support your wife.

Chapter 4: You Matter Too

There's a big focus on soon-to-be moms, and for the most part, the advice given to their partners can be summed up as "suck it up." Although that is true in some sense, you need to find a balance between when to man up and when to be kind to yourself.

Pregnancy is challenging for men because it is a highly stressful time. With all the "you're not the one growing a baby inside you," rhetoric doing the rounds, it's easy for men to feel guilty when they're finding it hard to deal with their stress or need to take time out just to relax.

You have to acknowledge that you're facing some issues of your own. You somehow need to be okay with seeing someone you love go from being a kind, loving, and rational person, to the total opposite. You have to shoulder more responsibility and put your wife first in every possible way. Gone are the days of relaxing after a busy day at the office; you have chores to do!

It's no wonder that pregnancy can be a real challenging time for men. If I'm honest, I struggled through both pregnancies. I had no idea how to manage my stress levels and this, I'm sad to say, did impact how supportive I could be to my partner. Let me share with you some things I did to relieve some of the pressure. It may not be easy to do but keep reminding yourself that you matter too.

Stick to a Routine

You're going to be busy and if you don't watch out, you will drown under the weight of your new chores. You will have to come up with a routine and stick to it as much as you can, if you want to fit all your new responsibilities into an already jam-packed day. Without a routine, you may get overwhelmed and end up doing nothing, and your wife will do it herself. To avoid her picking up the slack, plan ahead and keep to it.

Manage Your Responsibilities

You need to leave time to take care of yourself. If you're already barely coping with the responsibilities you have, see how you can lighten the load. For example, if you've been doing more than your fair share at work, consider having a chat with your boss to move some of your duties to someone else. Believe me, if they're a dad, they'll understand! Also, if the budget allows, outsource some of the chores around the house; get a gardener or a housekeeper once a week. Family and friends can also be helpful sources during this time, you just need to reach out.

Stand Up for Yourself

This is a hard one, but no one expects you to let your pregnant partner walk over you. Although you should do what you can to make life easier for your wife, it shouldn't come at your expense. You shouldn't be afraid to disagree with her or to stand up for yourself when she's being beyond unreasonable. Yes, her hormones are all over the place, but sometimes she just needs to be reminded that you're human too and also need support during this time. Don't sweat the small stuff, but speak up about things that really matter to you.

Blow Off Some Steam

You and your wife may benefit from some time apart, so take an hour here and there to do your own thing. Go to the gym or hang out with your buddies for a while; try to do something "normal" for a change to give your mind a break from thinking about your wife and your growing bundle of joy. Although this is a great way to reduce tension, you have to make sure you don't lose track of time and stay away from home for too long—that's just going to add to your stress levels.

These may seem like simple things to do, but it can be quite difficult to bring yourself to do it since your main focus is on your partner and your baby, and not yourself. But as I mentioned, you need to find ways to manage your stress levels or it may cause unnecessary disagreements and fights between you and your significant other. The main objective is to have as peaceful a pregnancy as possible, and to achieve that, your and her needs should both matter (even though hers should carry a little more weight).

It's true that you should "man up" and put your wife first during this time, but sometimes, manning up means putting yourself first for a while so that you can be the best version you can be for her while she's carrying your baby.

CONCLUSION

As we come to the end of this *Pregnancy Guide for Men: Preparing for Fatherhood Before Birth*, I hope you feel more at ease about what is lying ahead. There are going to be days filled with laughter, joy, and excitement about the future, but there are also going to be times when stress (and hormones) turn things sour.

The best advice I can give you is to take it day by day. You now have the skills to adapt your support strategy as you go; depending on how your wife is feeling any particular day. You also have access to a week-by-week breakdown of information that will prepare you for what's to come.

In the end, it all comes down to being a loving partner and father. How you treat your wife during the pregnancy says a lot about the type of dad you're going to be. So, start off right by making them the center of your world. But I have a feeling they already are!

Okay, Dada, Daddy, Pops, or maybe, Papi… I think your pregnant wife can do with a foot rub right about now, don't you?

Take care and congratulations on working toward being the best partner and parent you could possibly be.

If you found this book helpful, you may want to check out *Pregnancy Guide for Men: Navigating Postpartum Fatherhood* to help prepare you for life with a baby in the house.

References

Syndrome. (n.d.). Couvade syndrome. https://syndrome.org/couvade-syndrome/

Healthline. (2016). What does round ligament pain feel like: Symptoms, diagnosis, treatment. https://www.healthline.com/health/pregnancy/round-ligament-pain

Healthline. (2019). What do Braxton-Hicks feel like? https://www.healthline.com/health/parenting/what-do-braxton-hicks-feel-like

Book 2
Navigating the Newborn Phase

A Guide for New Dads
on the Journey of Fatherhood

INTRODUCTION

You nailed the challenge of being a supportive partner during your wife or significant other's pregnancy. You made it out on the other side alive, even though you at times may have feared for your life. Hormones can make a person crazy, right?

Now that your little one has joined the world, you may be wondering what next. You understood your role during pregnancy, but what now? Some of you may believe that your job is done; you can go back to your life before getting pregnant. That is not the case. You now have to do even more because you not only have a wife to support, but a tiny human to care for.

The two of you made this little miracle together and you can't expect your wife to shoulder all the responsibility. In other words, you will have to change your fair share of diapers and sacrifice your sleep for nightly feedings too.

I wrote this book with one aim: To help you step up to the role of father. If this is your first baby, you probably spent the last nine months of your life guessing and calculating what your wife needed. I know there were a few misses and things didn't always turn out as planned, but that was good preparation for what parenting is. None of us really know what we're doing; we just do our best and hope things work out in the end. Even the best parents out there fail at times.

My mother once told me something that took a lot of pressure off of me. She said if you're wondering whether you're a good parent, then you are because mothers and fathers who don't care for their children, won't second-guess themselves. So, here you are, holding a book meant to teach you how to care for your wife after giving birth and how to be a good dad to your newborn baby. Guess what, you're on the right track. You're making my job very easy—all I have to teach you is *how*; you already know *why* being a good partner and parent is important.

If you read my first book, *Pregnancy Guide for Men: Preparing for Fatherhood Before Birth*, then you know that it wasn't always smooth sailing for me. When my wife got pregnant the first time, I didn't know what to do so ended up doing next to nothing to support her. You can imagine the strain that put on our relationship. After our boy was born, the same thing happened; I was so overwhelmed with being responsible for a new life, that I fell into some kind of stupor and was unreliable during a time when my partner really needed me. I look back at that time with regret because I missed out on some key moments of our newborn's development. More than that, I made my wife feel alone.

After many fights and tears, I manned up and started to be a dad, and I am grateful to my wife for calling me out on my nonsense. I'm glad to say that the second pregnancy was much smoother, and after the birth of our daughter, I was present immediately— in body and mind.

If you follow the advice in this book, you'll prevent a lot of unnecessary heartache, and won't waste valuable time you have with your wife and bundle of joy as a family. I'm not saying it's going to be easy, but it is possible, and I know you have what it takes to make it work. Why? Because you're actually putting in the effort to get help to be a supportive partner and an amazing dad.

In this book, I'm going to walk you through the first few weeks after mommy and baby comes home. We'll look at what you can do to help your wife cope with the challenges of being a new mom—even though you're still figuring out the whole dad business yourself. You'll learn how to take care of a newborn so that you can give your wife a break, while you bond with your baby.

We don't have much time to waste; babies are very demanding, so we need to get your ready ASAP.

Chapter 1: The First Few Weeks

You know all about the first, second and third trimester—your wife just experienced them first-hand and you were along for the nine-month long ride. Saying there's another trimester may have caused you to break out in a sweat just a little, but you can relax. The fourth trimester is a way to make the world a little less scary for your little one. Just as you had to help your wife, you now have to be there for your baby as they adapt to the sights, sounds, smells, and sensations outside the womb.

Think of it this way, for nine months, your growing baby had a pretty cushy life. They didn't experience any hunger or thirst, painful bowel movements or stuck winds were a foreign concept, and they never had to experience feeling cold or hot. Your wife's womb was the perfect environment where they felt safe; close to mommy's heartbeat with all their needs catered for.

Then, suddenly, they're evicted and get bombarded with new experience after new experience. That's quite a shock and can be a very frightening time in your baby's life. In fact, it's going to take months for your baby to realize that mommy and them aren't one being. That's why the fourth trimester, which is basically just an extension of the third trimester but outside the womb, is so important.

The main idea behind the fourth trimester is to recreate an environment where your little one feels safe and soothed. Best yet, dads may not have wombs, but the fourth trimester gives them the opportunity to experience the closeness mom and baby had the previous nine months. How? Well, it's pretty easy actually.

Hold Them Close

When someone first told me to "wear my baby," I looked at them as if they were speaking a foreign language. Thank goodness my wife knew exactly what that meant and she handed me a baby sling. I loved the idea of having my little one so close to me, but I wasn't the only one benefiting from it; wearing your baby recreates quite a few conditions from the womb.

Your baby will feel:
- Supported as the sling holds them tight.
- Comforted because they can hear your heartbeat.
- Warm and cozy thanks to your body heat.

It's actually been found that babies cry and fuss 51% less when they're in a baby carrier or sling (Hunzikier & Ronald, 1986).

There's just one thing you have to remember. Don't let your baby face outwards; it's not good for their spine or hips. It's much better for them (and more special for you) if their chest touches yours.

Let Their Skin Touch Yours

There's nothing as great as taking a nap on a lazy Sunday afternoon, am I right? Well, to make it even better, bring your little one along for the Siesta and let their naked body cuddle up against your naked chest.

This level of closeness triggers oxytocin—the love and bonding hormone. Other benefits of skin-to-skin contact include:
- Maintaining the perfect body temperature.
- Maintaining the perfect heart rate, respiratory rate, and blood pressure.
- Boosting blood sugar levels.
- Reducing likelihood of crying.

If your wife is breastfeeding, your baby will be more likely to latch on and stay latched on for longer when there's no barrier between them. It will also be easier for your baby to show that they're ready to suckle if they have easy access to the nipple.

Take a Bath Together

Who doesn't like soaking in a nice warm bath? Although your baby may not enjoy it at first because they're not used to feeling cold air on their bare skin, they will soon grow to love spending time in the tub.

It can be scary when you first hold your baby in the bath. If this is the case, get in with them! You'll have the benefit of skin-to-skin contact while the warm water reminds them of their time in the womb, which will definitely make them happy.

Share Your Bed

Co-sleeping is all the rage at the moment and for good reasons. If this isn't your first child, you may already have experienced how your baby starts to cry as soon as you put them down for a nap in their cot. This happens because babies quickly feel vulnerable which triggers their danger alert system. The result: crying.

When you let your little one sleep in bed with you—close to mommy or daddy's skin—your baby will sleep better knowing that you're close-by. They will be able to smell you and can touch you when they start to feel panicky, which will prevent any crying.

I know this doesn't leave much room for romance in the bedroom. Welcome to parenthood, where your child determines when you and your wife can be intimate. If it's any consolation, it gets better as they grow older.

Wrap Them Up Nice and Tight

The womb is a pretty cramped space as birth approaches, but your baby felt great in their tiny, one-room apartment. They felt secure. To recreate that feeling outside the womb, try swaddling your baby. They will cry less and sleep better when they're wrapped tightly in a breathable cloth.

You may want to watch a video or ask a midwife to show you how to swaddle your baby. There are two important things you need to remember. First, don't wrap them too tight that you restrict their breathing. Second, leave their hips and legs room to move or they're at risk of hip dysplasia or dislocation.

That covers the fourth trimester, i.e., the first three months after the baby comes home. I, however, think that we should zone in a little more on specifically the first five days after birth, since those will be the most challenging.

Day 1

- Skin-to-skin contact is something you should focus on in the first 24 hours. Basically, whenever you or your wife hold your baby, there should be no barriers between you and them.

- Your baby will be hungry within an hour of birth, but your wife should have a steady supply of breastmilk going. If not, don't worry, formula milk is more than sufficient to nourish your baby.

- Although your little one will be hungry in the first hour, they will only need to drink 5-15 ml to feel content. Some babies are sleepers who will only need a few feeds on their first day, while others may want more. Your baby may suckle on mommy for 5-10 minutes or 20-30 minutes.

- Make sure you're there for your baby's first feedings if your wife is breastfeeding. Although breastfeeding is natural, there is a learning curve to it and your wife may feel embarrassed if she can't get your baby to latch. If this happens, remind her that it is both her and your baby's first time, so you're both still getting the hang of things. The more help she gets while in hospital, the more confident she'll feel breastfeeding at home.

- How your baby latches on to the nipple is important. Help your wife check the shape of her nipples after each feed. They shouldn't look squashed, flattened, ridged, or distorted in any way. If that happens, ask someone to help your wife hold the little one in the correct position while nursing.

- Are you ready for the first poop diaper? You're not. That is one thing I can tell you. The first poop is black or dark green, thick, and super sticky. This alien-looking poop is called meconium and is made from all the things your baby ingested while in the womb. So, brace yourself. Luckily, your baby will only pass meconium once or twice.

Day 2

- Your wife is going to be very tired on day two, and I'm sure you can do with some rest as well. Both of you should use the times your baby is sleeping to get some shuteye yourselves.

- Baby cuddles are essential on day two. Your baby is becoming more alert and aware of their surroundings, which can make them feel fearful. Keep them close as they get used to life outside of the womb.

- Your baby's appetite can increase quite significantly from day one; they may want to feed 10-12 times—day and night. That is going to put strain on your wife's nipples as she's getting used to being suckled. Have a chat with the nurse and ask her to recommend a nipple cream to help take some of the discomfort away.

- You have to count your baby's feedings. They need to nurse at least six times in 24 hours. If it is less, have a chat with your doctor so that they can check if everything is okay.

Day 3

- Your baby will instinctively know what they need to do to get you to produce more breastmilk. There may be times that they will want to nurse four to five times close together. This is called cluster feeding, and your wife may immediately think she's not producing enough milk and that is why your little one needs to feed so often. That's not the case. Cluster feeding is your baby's way to tell your wife's breasts, "Hey, I'm getting hungrier by the day, so you need to work harder."

- Have you noticed your baby examining your face as you hold them in your arms? That's because their eyes can focus on objects 50-60cm away—the distance between your face and theirs as you sway them in your arms. Remember, your baby knows you and your partner's voices; they've been hearing you talk for months. They're now linking the face with the person who talked to them so lovingly while they were still in mommy's tummy.

- It's not uncommon for parents to feel emotionally drained on day three. You've been through a lot the last couple of days or nine months depending how you look at it. Rest as much as you can. Also, I know your family members and friends are just as excited as you are and they can't wait to meet your little "mini-me," but for your and your wife's sake, try to limit visitors these first days. It is your time to get to enjoy your new baby.

Day 4

- It's possible that your wife and baby are still struggling to get breastfeeding just right. Keep rooting for them. Remind your wife that breastfeeding is a type of waltz; there are three sucking patterns she should look for. First, your baby will suckle quickly and in short bouts to draw the nipple back to the soft palate. This type of suckling can last for a few seconds. It's purely meant to trigger the release of milk and is non-nutritive. Second, your little on will stop sucking for a moment and then resume with strong deep sucks with short pauses in between. Since swallowing is still difficult, keep an eye and make sure that the suck and swallow ratio is 1/1. Third, the pauses will be longer followed by short bursts of deep sucking. You will notice your baby looking quite content during this suckling phase.

- If your wife is unsure when to switch breasts, you can let her know that she should allow unrestricted feeding on the first breast and only offer the second breast once your baby finishes. Don't worry if they don't want seconds, their tummy is probably full.

- You should expect around 4-6 wet nappies on day four. Their poop should now have the color of mustard and may contain small lumps.

Day 5

- Life outside the womb is becoming less scary. Your baby will be more settled in general and don't be surprised if you see a look of content on their little face, especially after a good feeding. That being said, there will still be times when your baby will need extra cuddles. But I know you're jumping at every chance you get to get closer to your child.

- If you're worried that holding your baby too often will spoil them, you can rest assured that it is not the case. Your little one has recently entered the bright, noisy, and cold world and they can do with a lot of comfort and reassurance.

- Poop alert! You may have to clean several poop diapers in one day. As long as your baby's stools are yellow-green and loose but not runny, then everything is a-okay.

Before we end this chapter, I want to talk a bit about what you may be feeling the first few days/weeks after your baby arrives in this world. There's a lot of focus on moms experiencing postpartum depression, but many don't know that anxiety and depression can affect dad's too at this time.

Dealing with Emotions

Those tiny fingers and cute little toes have stolen your heart. You have so much love for your baby it can be overwhelming at times. Still, you're an emotional mess at times, and you can't help but wonder why. The fact of the matter is that experiencing power emotions around the birth of a child is natural and doesn't have to be limited to only good feelings.

Life changing events always carry a risk of affecting people adversely. However, when it comes to your baby, guilt soon follows as you scold yourself for feeling anything but love and happiness. I know telling you that it's okay and you're only human won't do much to allay any guilt you may have.

It's not always easy to distinguish between anxiety, depression and stress and exhaustion. Your sense of "normal" isn't what it used to be; you've had to give up a lot of things and get used to others. Yes, you got a baby who you adore in return, but sometimes, our minds need to play catchup with reality.

To figure out if you're suffering from anxiety and depression or if you're just overly stressed and tired, below are some questions you can answer to give you a better idea. I'm also going to share the symptoms of anxiety and depression so that you can establish what's the cause for any negative feelings and deal with them appropriately.

Evaluate Your Risk for Depression and Anxiety

1. Have you ever had anxiety before, or have you been diagnosed with depression?
2. Does your wife have anxiety or depression?
3. Are you lacking a strong support system to lean on?
4. Are you stressed about finances?
5. Was the birth of your child difficult?
6. Have or are you addicted to alcohol or drugs?
7. Is your baby unhealthy?
8. Are you experiencing any other major life changes at the moment?
9. Is the reality of being a parent different than you imagined?

The more "yes" answers you give, the higher the likelihood of you having anxiety or depression.

Other factors that may contribute to the development of these mental health conditions, include:
- You're not able to bond with your little one.
- Bottling up your feelings and not asking for help because you don't want to be seen as a failure.
- Unwanted changes to your relationship with your wife.
- Stress relating to extra responsibilities, finances, or work.

Signs to Look Out For

It's time to take a close look at your feelings. How do you feel about your wife, your baby, and yourself? If many negative and pessimistic thoughts and feelings pop up, you may be experiencing anxiety or depression.

Symptoms of Depression

- You're super irritable and angry most of the time.
- Your mood is low, and you often feel sad and numb.
- You find yourself wanting to break out crying often.
- You feel hopeless about your future.
- You're not interested in your baby, partner, or other people or things you usually enjoyed.
- You're tired all the time.
- You find it hard to think clearly, can't concentrate, and your memory is not what it should be.

Symptoms of Anxiety

- Your worries consume you.
- You're on edge; constantly feeling irritated and restless.
- Your muscles are tense, and you may experience heart palpitations.
- You will have random outbursts of fear; panic attacks are common.

Dealing with the Baby Blues

It's clear that not only mommies experience some mental health struggles after birth. In this section, I'm going to share with you ways you can deal with your emotions. If you see your wife struggling with regulating her emotions, share these tips with her to help her get through difficult times.

The baby blues can leave you feeling sad and exhausted. In women, this partly happens due to hormonal changes; however, other factors such as exhaustion and stress also play a role. This is why men can experience it too. Usually, the baby blues doesn't linger for longer than one to two weeks, but to help you cope during that time, you should:

Sleep when you can: Not getting enough sleep can drive you mad. If you're helping with nightly feedings (as you should), then you need to find times to catch up on your sleep. You probably have a day job, which means you can't doze off when you feel like it—not that mom can either; she has to wait for the baby to nap before she can. Sit down with your wife and work out a feeding schedule. Personally, I enjoyed a two nights on, two nights off split, but find something that works for both of you. It truly is for the sake of your sanity.

Work as a team: Support each other. Both of you may be struggling with anxiety and depression, but when you shift the focus from yourself to your partner, you may end up feeling better. Helping others is good medicine. The only way to know how you can help your wife, is to ask her. In the same breath, she won't know you need help if you don't open up and tell her what is going on. Remember, you're a unit and should work together for the well-being of your family.

Plan some quality time with your baby: I previously mentioned the love hormone, oxytocin. Well, there's no way you can feel anxious or depressed if you boost your oxytocin levels by cuddling with a soft, warm, and loveable little angel. Hold your baby any chance you get. Even if you only feel better while they're in your arms, it's better than feeling miserable all the time.

I have to mention that your wife may have more than the baby blues. If her mood hasn't lifted in one to two weeks, she may have postpartum depression. This is more severe than the baby blues and takes a long time to go away. Some women get it two weeks after giving birth, while others only two months to a year later. If you think your wife may have postpartum depression, I recommend you contact your doctor, as suicidal ideations are common.

Symptoms to look for include:
- She wants nothing to do with your baby.
- She cries non-stop.
- Her appetite is gone.
- She doesn't take pleasure in anything.
- She often mentions that she can't cope.

- Her concentration is lacking, and she has many memory lapses.
- She gets panic attacks.
- She can't sleep and is extremely exhausted.

You should also consider post traumatic stress disorder if your wife had to endure a difficult or painful delivery.

This chapter covers the ups and downs of the first few weeks after the birth of your baby. You may notice that things aren't much easier than the previous nine months; they're just different issues you have to learn to deal with. But, I want you to remember that scattered in between the sleepless nights, dirty nappies, vomit, and crying, are special moments that will carry you through.

CHAPTER 2: BALANCING LIFE AND FATHERHOOD

It's easy to lose yourself when you're a dad. There are different hats you wear daily. When you go to work, you put on your "manger" hat, or "accountant" hat; when you get home and spend time with your baby, you're wearing your "dad" hat, and during times with your wife, your "husband" hat fits snuggly on your head. There are other hats like family, friend, colleague, etc.

The problem is that it can be challenging to take off your "dad" hat. If this happens, your whole life is consumed by your little one, and you lose yourself. That may sound like no big deal since it feels pretty great to have your world revolve around your baby, but in the long run, it's going to lead to unhappiness.

You will have to learn to juggle being a father with work, your relationships, and your personal wellbeing.

Here are some tips you can try to help you adjust to this new chapter of your life:

Take Some Time Off

Hopefully, you had a chat with your employer to see what the situation regarding your paternity leave is. If you're a U.S. citizen, companies are required by law to offer you 12 weeks' unpaid paternity leave. There are some companies who will still pay you a percentage of your salary during this time, so if you haven't yet, find out what your company's policies are.

If at all possible, I recommend you stagger your return to the office. You may have to use extra leave days, but it will make transitioning back to work a little less challenging. It is not a walk in the park trying to balance work and home, but staggering your return will make it easier. Speak to your boss and hear if you can start by working half days or maybe ask if you can work from home. I have to say, working from home is difficult unless you have an office out of earshot of your baby's cries. Even then, resisting the urge to go say "Hi" every few minutes may be a problem.

Work-Life Balance

Don't be surprised if your attitude toward work changes after having a baby. Where you once may have been a workaholic, you may now value time spent with family as important. Boring paperwork or baby cuddles? I think we all know which option will win.

Find out if there are ways you can make your work arrangements more flexible. Maybe you can go into work an hour later and skip lunch? What about only going to the office for half the day and working from home for the remainder? If you work for a family-friendly company, your boss may be willing to brainstorm with you.
If you're not lucky enough to be in a position to negotiate your work situation, you have to set boundaries. For example, if your boss is used to being able to reach you 24/7, things should change. Let him know that you'll only be in reach during office hours. Also, if you're often expected to work overtime because of an impossible workload, talk to your boss and make it clear that you will no longer be staying later or working during weekends.

For those dads who travel a lot for work, pre-record yourself reading bedtime stories. This will keep you connected to them even though you're far away. Then, when you're back, make the time to develop your bond.

Re-Classify Your Relationship

There's no doubt that the dynamic between you and your wife has changed. If this is your first child, you have to get used to it not just being the two of you any longer.

You and your partner have entered a new phase of your relationship and although this is great, it can be hard. The fact that being alone together is a rarity is a great example of the not-so-nice changes to your relationship. Being utterly exhausted when you finally can spend some time with your wife is another source of frustration.

You need to re-classify your relationship in your head—you're not a childless couple anymore and now have new responsibilities. Think of all the things you "lost" as a couple after having a baby, but then think of everything you've gained. This should give you some perspective.

Make time for each other. Take one day a week and make it date night. Get a babysitter and then go out to have some fun. Alternatively, drop your little one at Grandma's and stay in to cuddle on the couch while enjoying a movie. Most importantly, check in with each other; find out how you're both coping and what challenges you're facing and how the other person can help.

Take Care of Your Emotional Health

This is a big one. Your emotional state has an effect on your children and your wife. It's really important for you to find a way to relax and destress. The work-life balancing act we've talked about can be stressful, and when you add financial worries to the mix, your emotional health will suffer unless you do something.

You need to take time for yourself or you may find yourself growing resentful—feeling like your baby has taken over your life. Have a talk with your wife and come up with a plan where you two can still do things you enjoy. A good idea would be to take an hour over the weekend where you look after your baby alone and she can go out and do something fun. When she gets home, you can leave for an hour to recharge.

Other ways to look after your emotional health include:

Be Vulnerable

Cowboys don't cry, right? We've been raised to believe that men are rocks; we don't show what have been classified as "feminine" emotions. That's such an unhealthy way to approach life. Bottling up any emotions can lead to many mental health issues later on. If you're not one for sharing your feelings, now is the time to start. Tell your wife how you're feeling and what you're going through. She loves you and won't judge you for being vulnerable. Quite the opposite. She will probably love you even more and feel more inclined to share her struggles with you, which will ultimately bring you closer together.

Learn to Let Go

Don't laugh, but I am going to quote an animation movie—when your baby becomes a toddler, you'll understand how it is possible to memorize quotes from a movie.

In Kung Fu Panda, there is this wise old turtle called Master Oogway. He said:

"Yesterday is history, tomorrow is a mystery, and today is a gift. That is why it is called the present."

One of the main reasons why our emotional health declines is because we either cling to the past or obsess and worry about the future. For your own sanity, you have to learn to live in the present. Let go of what happened; you can't change the past, and stop dreaming up worst-case scenarios about the future.

Enjoy the gift of the present with your wife and baby.

Get to Know Yourself

Who are you and what do you want out of life? Self-awareness is key to emotional health, so take some time to get to know yourself. The more comfortable you are with yourself, you'll find it easier to approach life with openness, acceptance, and honesty, and, in the end, you'll lead a more fulfilling life. It takes courage to take a deep dive into who you are, but if you don't, you're going to run on autopilot and that is no way to live—and your mind will tell you that as your emotional health declines.

The Nitty Gritty

I think it is time we take care of some practicalities. I have no doubt that the questions below have crossed your mind before and maybe still appear in a flash of panic every now and again. So, let's arm you with some baby-raising knowledge so you can earn the title of "super dad."

How often and how much should my baby eat?
You have to keep in mind that your little one's stomach is super tiny. As you read earlier, in the beginning, 5-10ml is all they need. That is because their stomach is the size of a marble on day one and two, and then grows to the size of a large egg on day 10, and so on. You want your baby to look content after giving them the bottle. Usually, if they don't want to drink anymore, they will turn their head away from the teat.

How do I make them a bottle?
There are many reasons why you and your wife may decide to bottle feed. It can be a case of her running out of milk. Of course, she may pump out breast milk so that you can get up to feed the little rascal at night so she can get some sleep. It doesn't matter why your baby is drinking out of a bottle and what (milk or formula) they're drinking; all you have to worry about is that the liquid is the right temperature. There are gizmos out there that keep the bottles at the right temperature, but that isn't a great idea if it is breast milk. Other methods to heat the water include boiling some water and putting the bottle inside the par-boiled water for a minute or two. You can also place it in the microwave for a few seconds. Still, how are you supposed to feel how hot it is on the inside? There's this age-old trip of dripping some of the milk, straight out of the bottle onto your wrist. Although this does work, keep in mind that what is lukewarm to you, may be hot to your little one. I suggest you get a food-grate thermometer to check that the milk is around 98.5 degrees Fahrenheit.

Ask your wife to show you during the day, but pay attention! You don't want to have to wake her up at 3 am to ask, "How many scoops of formula?"

How Many Dirty Diapers Can I Expect?
Too many. Heaps the size of mountains, or that is what it will feel like. On day one,

your baby should have at least one poop diaper, this should increase to five to six on day six or seven. It gets worse, at the end of week one, your cute little baby will turn into a poop machine and you'll have to stand ready to change their diaper one to 12 times a day!

Just know that the poop of a breastfed baby and a formula-fed baby are different in color and consistency. Formula-fed babies poop less, but their stools are larger, more formed, and the color of chocolate. The poop color from breastfed babies varies and depends on mom's milk. In the beginning as your wife's milk changes from colostrum to milk, the stool will go from green to tan to mustard colored.

How Do I Change a Diaper?
If you have a boy, the biggest tip I can give you is to keep their penis covered with some part of the diaper while you're cleaning his bump and positioning the new diaper. Trust me, they turn into peeing Cherub fountains as soon as their privates are exposed to cold air.

For girls, the most important thing is to wipe from front to back. You don't want any stool to get into her genital area as she may get an infection.

Don't let your baby wear a wet or dirty diaper for too long. Not only are they likely to develop a rash, but it may also be harder to potty train them later on.

You shouldn't worry too much. Before you know it, you'll have a whole system going.

My wife asked me to pack a diaper bag. Help!
A diaper back is a magical invention—if your wife packs it! Without supervision the first few times and thorough instructions, you will likely forget important things that you can't go without. My wife made me a list of what should always be packed and she attached it to the diaper bag itself. All I need to do is pack item for item and we can both rest assured that no essentials were left behind.
Here's a list you can use but ask your wife if she wants to add anything to it!

Remember to pack:

- Diapers
- Wipes
- Rash cream
- Two sets of clothes (one warm and one for hotter weather)
- A swaddle blanket
- A burp rag
- A bag to transport dirty diapers back home
- Bottles
- Formula
- Water
- Extra pacifier
- Hand sanitizer
- A toy or two

Extra Tips for Hands-On Dads

We've covered many things in this chapter that will make you a better dad while continuing to look after your own wellbeing as well.

I want to now share with you some helpful hints I picked up along the way. They're simple but have effective results.

Turn your forearm into a pillow. When you cradle your little one in your arms, they may be constantly looking for a breast. Since that is mom's department, flip your little one over and hold them face down on your arm. Their little face can nuzzle into the inside of your forearm, while your hand holds them steady under their crotch. It is like your forearm was built to be a pillow for a newborn!

Audition for the Daddy Idols. Sing to your little one. It doesn't matter if you hold a tune or not, just do it. You will have your baby's undivided attention and they will respond to your voice.

Do it alone. I know it is scary to be alone with your little one without mommy hovering over your shoulder, but you can do it. You don't need someone to bail you out. If you're apprehensive and afraid your baby is going to cry the whole time they're alone with you, pinpoint times during the day when they're their happiest. After nursing and being burped is also a good time to learn to go it alone. You'll become more confident in time.

Don't take things personally. Moms are like wild bears protecting their young. You have to accept the fact that she may not have confidence in your skills as a dad. She's probably constantly questioning her own parenting abilities, as well. So, to try to take control of a situation where she feels out of control, she may correct you or want things done her way and her way only. You have to develop a thick skin, or you will be at each other's throats. This will only last until both your parenting skills increase and she trusts you (and herself).

We've come to the end of Chapter 3, and I hope you have a better idea how to be a dad without neglecting your wants and needs. Your priorities in life have changed; in fact, many things in your life have changed. Don't try to force your life with a newborn into an old mold. When you adapt to your new life, it will be much easier for you to balance the different hats you have to wear.

Although we touched on ways you can bond with your little one briefly in previous chapters, it is time to make that our sole focus now. Don't believe that the depth of connection or attachment mom and baby have are unattainable. You just have to work at it a little harder because you don't have the history of physically carrying your growing baby inside of you. But don't worry, I've got you. I'm going to share with you everything you can do to form a deep and lasting bond with your little one.

CHAPTER 3: BOND WITH YOUR BABY

It's normal for you to be concerned about your relationship with your baby. I'm not going to beat around the bush—it's the primary caretaker who has the strongest bond with the baby (in the early years). But that doesn't mean your connection with your little one can't be strong. If you're not a stay-at-home dad, you'll just have to work a little harder to build a deep bond with your baby.

One thing is certain, whether your little one has the best relationship with their mommy or daddy, they should have a secure attachment with someone! Without an attachment bond, your child won't develop as well as they can intellectually, socially, and emotionally. In essence, attachment is a key factor in brain development.

The bond you have with your baby can be either good or bad. That's good news for you because you don't have to wade through gray waters to get to where you want to be.

The foundation of a *secure* attachment bond is safety and understanding. If you can consistently make your little one feel safe and peaceful through understanding what they want and need, and who they are, you're on the right track. You're not able to build a bond with your baby through conversation; they can't share their life story with you for you to be able to find common ground and grow attached. A secure attachment bond is an entirely wordless emotional exchange. When your baby has such a bond with someone (or hopefully many someones), their nervous system will develop to its full potential; they'll be more eager to learn in the future, be more self-aware, and will have consideration for others.

If we look at an *insecure* attachment bond, we'll see that parents don't offer their infant safety, support, and acceptance. This will create a lot of confusion in that little mind of theirs and they will struggle to form their own identity, and find it difficult to learn and relate to others.

So, now that you know what to do and not to do, let's look at how you can go about fostering a secure attachment bond between you and your newborn.

It's pretty simple, actually. The more you interact with your baby in a way that makes them feel safe and understood, the deeper your bond will grow. This is true even in the first days of your baby's life. They start reading your emotional cues pretty soon after entering this world. They'll pay attention to your tone of voice, gestures, and can sense big emotions like happiness and anger. What's great is that they'll respond to you; they'll coo, mimic your expressions, and cry. Later on, they'll smile, laugh, point, or yell in response to your emotions.

You also need to pay attention to their cues and respond accordingly. Their wants are pretty straightforward the younger they are: food, warmth, and affection. When you can successfully pick up on their cues and fulfill the associated need, and do so continuously, then a secure attachment bond is guaranteed. Of course, you are going to misread some of the cues, but don't stress, babies don't hold grudges!

Before we get to the tips, let's have a closer look at why secure attachment is important, because, often, parents struggle to make the link between how a relationship can impact the development of an organ or system. I'm not going to get all *sciency*, but you have to remember that everything you do will affect how your baby develops. Your actions will create pathways in their brain and make neurons fire in a certain way. Remember, the brain is like a computer's motherboard—everything runs through it and the available pathways will direct the actions. In other word, if you want your child to have a healthy sense of self but there aren't any pathways leading to that goal, you'll have to help create them through your actions and guidance, or they'll have to do it themselves when they're older and realize, "Oh, I don't really know who I am and what I'm doing here."

Secure attachment makes the brain grow in all the right parts if you want to raise a loving, understanding, empathetic, and approachable child. Your little one will also, in future, be able to:

- Have more fulfilling intimate relationships.
- Practice emotional regulation.
- Have higher confidence.
- Enjoy spending time with others.
- Be more resilient and recover from disappointment and loss quicker.
- Share how they feel.

But it doesn't end there; secure attachment is good for parents, as well.

Many parents describe their deepening relationship with their child as "falling in love." That is a very good description because it does really feel like that as you and your baby grow more attached. We again have the love or cuddle hormone oxytocin to thank for this joy we experience as we connect with our little one. The elation you feel from your relationship with your little one will relieve some of the fatigue you have thanks to all those late-night feedings. You'll be more motivated, have more energy, and feel over the moon the deeper your bond with your baby is.

Okay, I'm sure you're burning to know how to bond with your baby. Just remember that it's not going to happen overnight. Stay patient with yourself as you try to take your baby's cries, coos, and other cues and turn them into an understandable "language." With time, it will become easier to know exactly whether your baby is asking for cuddles, comfort, food, or a nap.

Tips for Creating Secure Attachment

It starts with you. You won't be able to accurately read your baby's cues and respond accordingly if you're overwhelmed, sleep deprived, and in a bad space emotionally. They say, "You can't pour from an empty cup," and that is precisely what I mean. Since building a secure attachment with your baby depends on fulfilling their needs, you need to make sure you actually have the energy to do it.

Get enough sleep: I am the worst person when I don't get enough sleep. I'm cranky and super irritable. I know I'm not alone. Sleep deprivation turns most of us into grumpy old men (and women). You will have to come up with a nightly feeding schedule that will benefit you and your wife. Don't feel bad if you try it one way and it doesn't work; keep looking for a routine where you won't end up feeling like you've been hit by a train every day of the week.

Ask for help: You and your wife are partners. You're raising your baby together, so don't be scared to ask for their help. Yes, she already has a lot to do, but if you're pulling your weight, then so do you. On days that you really can't cope, let her know. I'm sure she wouldn't mind shouldering some extra responsibilities to make you feel better. Just know, she may need you to help her out in the future! You can also ask friends or family to help out, so that both of you can take a breather.

Set aside some "me" time: Caring for a newborn is hard work. The only time your baby won't need your full attention is when they're taking a nap, and usually you'll use that time to get some rest yourself. When will you have time to do the things you love doing? Well, you'll have time if you make time. To be a more effective parent, taking an hour to recharge in whatever way you like will give you perspective.

When you find yourself spiraling out of control because your basic needs aren't being met, then you may want to find ways to calm yourself before interacting with your little one. Remember, your baby can't communicate verbally; they build their image of you on your emotional reactions, and will adapt their responses to those cues. For example, if you're anxious to bottle-feed your baby, you're probably not going to have much success as your baby will feel a little flustered themselves. Similarly, if you try to soothe your baby but your mood screams agitated, then you can forget that they'll stop fussing and calm down.

So, when you find your emotions are on a roller-coaster ride, try this:

- Breathe. Deeply. You may have to let your little one cry a little longer while you compose yourself. Take a deep breath or a few if you need to, and then you can try to calm your baby.

- Play tag-team. If you're feeling flustered and out of control, ask your wife to take control of the current situation. This will give you time to reign in your emotions, so you can continue to be a compassionate and caring dad.
- Go for a walk. There's nothing like fresh air to soothe your soul. An environmental change can also take the edge off if you're having a particularly stressful time with your baby.

You have to prepare for the worst because I can tell you now, there are going to be days when you're so frazzled, you won't recognize yourself and your emotional regulation will go out the window. It's nothing to feel guilty over. You're human and you're running on empty, so give yourself a break. As long as you do what you can to prevent your little one from bearing the brunt of your bad day, then all is well.

Attachment Tip 1: Learn Your Baby's Cues

Each baby is unique; they have their own personality and preferences. Even if this is your second or third child, you will still have to learn your baby's cues and how they want you to respond to them. For example, one baby may be peaceful and calm in a noisy environment, while another baby needs peace and quiet for them to relax and be okay.

You'll get a lot of advice from well-meaning family and friends. They'll tell you what worked for their baby, thinking it will work for yours, as well. It may or it may not, and nothing is stopping you from trying it, but don't try to force what worked for them onto your little one.

You will have to figure out what your baby wants, and since they can't talk, it's basically a process of illumination. For the foreseeable future, you're going to be a sensory detective. It's up to you to recognize what each sound, facial expression, or bodily movement means. This is quite challenging as, at first, all of their coos and cries will sound the same. But, believe me, they're all entirely unique.

To help you learn your little one's cues:

- Pay attention to their face and body movements. For example, your baby may squirm around and move their arms around in the air when they hear you talk,

71

all in an attempt to get you to pick them up and cuddle them so they can steal some of your body heat.

- Listen closely to the sounds they make. My daughter used to wail when she was hungry, but when she was tired, her cry was more low-pitched and it came in these short bursts. Of course, it took me a while to figure that out, but I can tell you, when I did, things became significantly easier.

- Find out what type of touch your baby finds pleasurable. Some babies prefer firmer pressure while others like a gentler touch. The sooner you can figure this out, the easier it will be for you to handle your baby. Remember, your little one's senses are taking in every aspect of their environment and through that, they form a picture of the world. If you want to show your baby that the world is a loving and comforting place, then you have to show them in a language they understand.

- Take note of how your baby reacts to certain movements, sounds, and surroundings. My friend's newborn boy falls asleep in an instant when driving in the car with metal music blasting over the speakers. If I had to do that with one of my children, they would scream non-stop. Like I mentioned earlier, it is about trial and error; don't be afraid to think out of the box.

Throughout the process of building secure attachment with your baby, remind yourself of one thing: There are times your baby will fuss no matter what. When they're sick, teething, or going through a growth-spurt, they will be impossible to handle. All you need to do when this happens is to keep communicating and figuring out how you can meet their needs. If you stay patient and treat them with love and compassion throughout their continuous fussing, they'll start to learn that you love them unconditionally.

Attachment Tip 2: No One Likes A "Hangry" Baby

Have you ever been so hungry that you're angry? Well, that's what is called "hangry," and it isn't a good emotional state to be in as everything around you just seems wrong! Much the same happens when someone doesn't get enough sleep. Wait, I don't have to tell you anything about that, right? You have first-hand experience.

Your baby experiences the same emotions when they're hungry or sleepy, which will make them extra difficult to pacify. They will have a hard time engaging and interacting with you when they're in this mode, which can be a great source of frustration to both of you. So, make sure your little one gets frequent feedings and enough rest if you want to successfully work on deepening your bond.

In the first few months, babies need to sleep 16-18 hours a day. If they're getting less sleep than that, their behavior will be frenzied, and they may look hyper-alter. Don't mistake this as an invitation to play; it's just their way of telling you that they should've been napping already. It's not often that babies fall asleep spontaneously, so if that is what you're waiting for to happen, you're going to have one tired and irritable baby in your arms.

When it comes to feeding, you have to take growth spurts and development changes into consideration when planning a schedule. If you see your baby is hungry more often than work in extra feedings to keep them happy. Your baby's body is great at telling you what they want and need, you just need to decipher it all!

Attachment Tip 3: Talk, Love, Play

It's important to have fun with your baby and spend quality time together. Sharing laughter and smiles with your baby is as important as food and sleep. If you see your baby is ready for a play session, drop everything you're doing, and interact with them.

I know you may feel uncomfortable and self-conscious acting silly with your baby, but get over it. I always joke that it is time to let out my inner child, but that is exactly what you need to do. It may feel awkward in the beginning but seeing the joy on your baby's face and hearing those happy gurgles will make it all worth it.

At this age, a simple game of peek-a-boo or making funny faces can lead to long periods of entertainment. Just be mindful that your little one can become overstimulated quite quickly, so while you're having fun, keep an eye on their body language. If you don't, things can go from fun and laughter to chaos and tears in a split second.

Even if you're not actively playing with them and they're just doing their own thing, talk to them. My wife talks to our kids constantly. The sound of her voice soothes them, but it will also help their language development later on.

Attachment Tip 4: Don't Try to be Perfect

Repeat after me: "The perfect parent doesn't exist." No one can be perfect all the time. Yes, you'll have your moments where you can pat yourself on the back and say, "Good job," but aiming for perfection all the time is exhausting and unattainable.

You won't always know what your baby wants, and there will be days when even if you do know, you may take a little longer to give it to them. That's okay. Secure attachment is about the quality and awareness of the interaction, and your willingness to notice when you missed a signal and find a way to fix it.

Understanding your little one's cues half of the time already makes you a great parent, and even though I know you're going to aim for much more than that, I hope you're not too hard on yourself if you misread a cue or two. It's impossible to be present and attentive 24 hours a day, so stop trying. You're going to miss out on so many great moments if you keep focusing on what you did wrong and not acknowledging what you did right.

Challenges to Bonding with Your Baby

Not everything is in your control and at times, there can be an obstacle in your way to building a secure relationship with your child. This doesn't mean you won't be able to create a secure attachment at all, it just means the process will be delayed and may get interrupted ever so often.

Although most babies are born ready to soak up all the love they can get and connect with their primary caregivers, sometimes there are problems that get in the way. These include:
- A compromised nervous system
- Problems during pregnancy or during birth
- Health issues

- Premature birth where they had to spend their first hours/days in intensive care

The sooner you identify possible problems, the easier it will be for you to overcome them. You can have a chat with your pediatrician if any of the above applies to your little one. They will be able to point you in the right direction and give you some helpful tips.

For you as a parent, you may have trouble connecting with your little one due to:
- Depression, anxiety, or other mental health conditions.
- Drug or alcohol use and abuse.
- Stress
- A history of abuse or neglect as a child
- Negative childhood experiences and memories
- Growing up in an unsafe environment

The good news is that all of this can be overcome. If you put in the work, you can have a wonderful bond with your baby that will grow deeper as your child grows. Setting the right foundation when they're still young, will make your life as a parent much easier when they reach teenage years.

As a father, I hope you now realize you can have a special bond with your baby too; it's not just something reserved for mothers. In fact, not to toot my own horn, but my youngest actually has a much deeper bond with me than their mother. No, it's not a competition, but I want you to know that you matter to your child. You just have to show them that they matter to you.

CONCLUSION

You're well on your way to becoming a successful and accomplished father. You now have all the important information you need to win the "Dad of the Year" award.

You probably realize that being a parent is all about finding balance. Balance between work and home; balance between feeding your baby too much or too little; balance between spending time alone and as a family, and so on. However, to get the equilibrium just right, you are going to have to put in some work. Parenting is a learning curve, and you can't sit back and believe it will come naturally.

If you want to be a good parent, you need to educate yourself about how to raise a well-adjusted child, but you also need to learn more about yourself. As you go on a journey of self-discovery, you may notice some toxic parenting traits you have that were caused by your parents. Knowing the effect it has on you, you can actively work toward breaking the cycle and becoming a more involved and loving father.

As I mentioned in the Introduction, I want you to step up to the role of father. This may sound easy, but it isn't. It's not as straightforward as just stepping up. Why? Because what is classified as a good father? To some people, a father is someone who provides and that's it. To others, a father is someone who is emotionally available. You have to answer this question yourself, and then have a chat with your wife and ask her if she agrees. Only once you know what you want to be, will you be able to work toward it. Even then, it's going to be hit and miss. None of us know what we're doing; we all stumble and fall, rethink our approach and adapt. If you're a good parent, you're constantly trying to improve.

The advice in this book will take you one step closer to being a dad your child will look up to one day; a dad your child will thank for loving them and caring for them so deeply.

I want to thank you for trying to do and be better. Fathers have a bad reputation, but it's through people like you that we'll start to break the stereotype of dads being deadbeats.

If you want to help the cause of rewriting the narrative of fathers, please recommend this book to others. Leaving a favorable review will also be much appreciated. Good luck ahead, but I don't think you need much luck, you have love and the determination to be a superstar dad to drive you!

References

Hunziker, U.A. & Barr, R.G. (1987). Increased carrying reduces infant crying: A randomized controlled trial. Pediatrics, 77 (5): 641–648. https://doi.org/10.1542/peds.77.5.641

Printed in Great Britain
by Amazon